LONDON TRANSPORT in Colour
1950-1969

Kevin McCormack

Ian Allan
PUBLISHING

Introduction

This colour album covers the transport activities of London Transport (LT) during the 1950s and 1960s (and also contains a shot from 1939!). However, it gives a broader perspective than my previous LT albums because, as well as featuring buses, trolleybuses and even a few trams, it is the first to include the Underground.

With my interest in British Railways (BR) in steam days, I had a particular affection for the Metropolitan (Met) Line from Baker Street to Aylesbury and made a point of travelling on the special train which ran on the last day, 9 September 1961, hauled by Bo-Bo No 18 *Michael Faraday* and then by 2-6-4 tank No 42070. My enthusiasm for this line was doubtless due to the fact this was the closest the Underground came to being a main-line operation, and steam haulage was involved. Furthermore, much as I normally despised diesels and electrics, I was attracted to the Met Bo-Bo locomotives, primarily because of their archaic appearance and age (almost 40 years old by the time I came to know them, around 1959). Designed to haul 180-ton passenger trains from Baker Street to Harrow-on-the-Hill in 15 minutes, they were impressively powerful — and sounded it when running in confined places like Baker Street and Liverpool Street. Then there was the slam-door rolling stock, both the examples which were locomotive-hauled (the 'Dreadnoughts') and the multiple-units ('T' stock). Both types were anachronisms by the time they entered the 1960s, none more so than the Chesham stock, which comprised surely the last standard-gauge Victorian carriages to run in everyday service in Britain (and are still running today in preservation on the Bluebell Railway). LT also had a fleet of steam engines, by this time confined to miscellaneous duties but which, as a result of their nocturnal activities on track-maintenance trains, gave rise to much speculation in the press that there were 'ghost trains' on the Underground!

Continuing the LT railway theme, I have included some more conventional Underground trains from other lines. Also I have focussed on two branch lines which have ceased operation, namely Acton Town– South Acton (rarely seen in colour) and Epping–Ongar (which has reopened as a privately operated heritage line).

With regard to road transport content, I have once again been fortunate to find some new colour material of LT vehicles, which will enable readers to appreciate London and its environs in less frenetic days. In addition to including some general material, I have concentrated on two themes not covered in depth in my previous LT titles — red buses working on Country Area (green) routes to the south of the capital and trolleybus operations to the east of London.

I am very grateful, as ever, to the photographers who have kindly provided material — Marcus Eavis, Roy Hobbs, Neil Davenport, Phil Tatt, Nick Lera, Dave Brown, C. Carter, Harry Luff, David Hurdle, Jim Oatway and the late Mike Harries. The photographs taken by the late Jack Wyse are reproduced by courtesy of the London Branch of the Light Rail Transit Association, and those from the Online Transport Archive — a registered charity caring for photographic collections — by courtesy of Martin Jenkins.

Now it's time for another sentimental journey by London Transport.

Kevin R. McCormack
Ashtead, Surrey
January 2005

First published 2005
Reprinted 2006

ISBN (10) 0 7110 3073 1
ISBN (13) 978 0 7110 3073 2

Published by Ian Allan Publishing

an imprint of Ian Allan Publishing Ltd, Hersham, Surrey KT12 4RG.
Printed by Ian Allan Printing Ltd, Hersham, Surrey KT12 4RG.

Code: 0606/3

Title page: Sidcup garage's RT2756 and Plumstead's RT882 display contrasting body types as they stand at Bexleyheath trolleybus depot, the northern/eastern terminus of their respective routes, in 1958. *Phil Tatt*

Front cover: In the rush hour some through services ran between Baker Street and Chesham — a duty which in 1961, when this photograph was taken at Chesham, enabled the Bo-Bo electric locomotives to work alongside the new 'A60' stock which by that time had taken over the branch service. No 16 *Oliver Goldsmith* would shortly move its train of 'Dreadnought' stock to the platform road for the return journey to Neasden. *Marcus Eavis*

Above: A four-car set of clerestory-roofed 'Q' stock headed by a former 'G'-class motor car of 1923 leaves Kew Gardens on the District Line in 1958. An electric unit working the BR Broad Street–Richmond service stands at the adjacent platform. *Marcus Eavis*

3

Above: Fairburn 2-6-4 tank No 42279 stands at Aylesbury in the summer of 1961 with a set of 'Dreadnought' coaches. In 1937 responsibility for providing steam haulage for LT trains on the Rickmansworth–Aylesbury section was transferred from LT to the London & North Eastern Railway (LNER). BR inherited this function in 1948, which it performed until 9 September 1961; after that date the Metropolitan Line was cut back to Amersham — the extremity of the electrification extension from Rickmansworth — beyond which BR became the sole operator. *Marcus Eavis*

Right: In 1958 BR's London Midland Region became responsible for providing steam motive power on LT trains beyond Rickmansworth in place of the Eastern Region. Midland motive power was already in evidence on 2 June 1957, when this photograph of Fairburn tank No 42253, preparing to leave for Aylesbury, was taken at Rickmansworth. As usual, the engine is coupled to a set of 'Dreadnought' coaches, three of which have been preserved by the Keighley & Worth Valley Railway in Yorkshire. *Neil Davenport*

Left: Electric locomotives Nos 11 *George Romney* and 18 *Michael Faraday* stand in the sidings at Rickmansworth in summer 1958 ready to haul LT through trains from Aylesbury back to Baker Street or Liverpool Street. Electrification to Amersham was completed in September 1960, but through trains to Aylesbury continued for a further year. *Marcus Eavis*

Above: Metropolitan Line trains terminating at Rickmansworth or Watford, where there was no steam leg involved, did not require locomotive-hauled carriages and were operated by 'T'-class compartment stock dating from 1927-32. This view at Northwood was recorded in 1959, just before quadrupling of the track between Harrow-on-the-Hill and the junction with the Watford branch, one mile north of Moor Park. *Marcus Eavis*

Above: A steel-panelled motor car from the last batch of 'T' stock dating from 1932, attached to earlier 'T'-stock trailers, leaves Rickmansworth for Aldgate. Locomotive-hauled stock bound for Aylesbury is standing in the platform. 'T' stock survived to run on the electrification extension to Amersham, their passenger service career ending on 5 October 1962. *Marcus Eavis*

Right: Early 'T' stock bound for Watford prepares to leave Wembley Park on 1 October 1961. The twin parallel wires above the train were used to enable the guard to give the starting signal to the driver. The furled flag seen here had a brass boss on the end to short circuit the wires and sound a bell. *Nick Lera*

Electric locomotive No 3 *Sir Ralph Verney* stands at Northwood in summer 1959. The Metropolitan Railway had main-line ambitions to extend northwards but never reached beyond Verney Junction, on the Bletchley–Oxford line. The LPTB considered that the Met already extended too far from London, so it proceeded to close the uneconomic Quainton Road–Brill branch in 1935 and pulled back from Verney Junction to Aylesbury in 1936. *Marcus Eavis*

The Watford branch opened in November 1925 as a joint venture between the Metropolitan Railway and the LNER and was electrified from the outset. This 1959 view at Watford depicts 'T' stock, which was specifically designed to provide a fast through service from Baker Street. *Marcus Eavis*

Left: In 1932 the Metropolitan Railway opened its branch to Stanmore, where Class E 0-4-4 tank No L44 was photographed working a railtour on 1 October 1961. This locomotive was built by the Metropolitan Railway at Neasden Works in 1896 and is now preserved as Metropolitan No 1 at the Buckinghamshire Railway Centre at Quainton Road. The Met's main-line passenger steam locomotives were transferred to the LNER in 1937, but smaller types such as the 'E'-class tanks, which had also been used for passenger work (notably on the Chesham branch), were retained for miscellaneous duties. *Marcus Eavis*

Above: Electric locomotive No 8 *Sherlock Holmes* approaches Rickmansworth in 1961 with an Aylesbury train. This engine was the last of its class to retain Metropolitan Railway crimson livery, losing it in the summer of 1939, and was also the first to regain this livery, together with replacement nameplates, in October 1953. Twenty of these locomotives were built, in 1921/2, and, due to the deferral of electrification beyond Rickmansworth, the surviving 16 locomotives were overhauled and returned to their former glory from 1953. *Marcus Eavis*

Above: Watched by a boy scout, electric locomotive No 4 *Lord Byron* enters Rickmansworth station on 2 June 1957. Standard 2-6-4 tank No 80140, barely a year old, has just been taken off a train from Aylesbury. Metropolitan Railway electrification from Baker Street started in 1906, when the change to/from steam was effected at Wembley Park. The changeover point moved to Harrow-on-the-Hill in 1908 and then to Rickmansworth in 1925. *Neil Davenport*

Right: This rural view dating from 2 June 1957 depicts one of the two three-car push-and-pull sets used on the Chalfont & Latimer–Chesham branch until the line was electrified and steam operation replaced from 12 September 1960. The carriages, which are still in varnished teak, are being propelled by an ex-Great Central Railway 'C13'-class 4-4-2 tank. *Neil Davenport*

Above: The Chesham sets consisted of Ashbury-built former steam stock dating from 1898-1900 which, following the introduction of larger carriages and progressive electrification, had been converted into electric multiple-units from 1906. Six vehicles were subsequently re-converted to steam stock to make two sets for the Chesham branch. One such set is seen here in the bay platform at Chalfont & Latimer as a Marylebone–Aylesbury local train pulls away. *Neil Davenport*

Right: Devoid of its nameplate (removed for the war effort) and carrying instead the LT fleetname on a wooden board, Met electric locomotive No 1 *John Lyons* is detached from an Aylesbury-bound train at Rickmansworth on 27 March 1954. After the London Passenger Transport Board (LPTB) absorbed the Metropolitan Railway in 1933 the crimson livery gave way to the grey-and-red livery shown here, but crimson was reintroduced, along with replacement nameplates, from 1953. *Neil Davenport*

Left: Within a short time four of the six Chesham carriages would be filled with smiling Bluebell Railway passengers instead of these miserable commuters waiting to leave Chalfont & Latimer station in 1960. The standard Metropolitan Railway round-top doors seen here on coach Nos 515 and 518 (which by this time had lost their varnished-teak livery) were designed to minimise damage if opened when the train was in a tunnel with limited clearances. *Marcus Eavis*

Above: Electric locomotive No 5 *John Hampden* (now preserved, along with No 12 *Sarah Siddons*) hauls a special train of 'Dreadnought' stock (built between 1910 and 1923) into Amersham station on 26 May 1963 as part of the Metropolitan centenary celebrations. 'A60' stock (remarkably still in use today) had taken over from the electric locomotives in September 1961, but a few of the old locomotives were retained for miscellaneous non-passenger duties. *Marcus Eavis*

Left: LT put on a magnificent display at Neasden depot in May 1963 to commemorate the Metropolitan centenary. The exhibits depicted in this view consist of Class E 0-4-4 tank No L44, Bo-Bo locomotive No 1 *John Lyon* and sets of 'T' and 'F' stock. *Author*

Above: Retained for the centenary exhibition and broken up shortly after, L52 was one of four Metropolitan Railway Class F 0-6-2 tanks built by the Yorkshire Engine Co in 1901 for freight work and was originally numbered 93. *Marcus Eavis*

Above: In 1956 LT set about replacing its aging steam locomotives with ex-Great Western Railway pannier tanks, eventually buying 13 from BR. This view shows L94 (ex-GWR No 7752 and now preserved) at Neasden shed. The last three were withdrawn in May 1971. *Author*

Right: While most of LT's steam locomotives were based at Neasden, a few were kept at Lillie Bridge, on the District Line near Earl's Court. There is no shortage of variety in this view, with L54 (ex-Met No 102, built by Peckett in 1899), an ex-District Railway 0-6-0 tank built by Hunslet in 1931 (behind the coal wagon) and pannier tank L91. *Jim Oatway*

Left: On 3 October 1965 bus routes 409, 410 and 411 became the first LT Country Area services to receive Routemasters. The intention was to use a batch of new RMLs (all earlier Routemasters being red-painted buses or Green Line coaches), but for various reasons there were insufficient green vehicles available on this date. Consequently Godstone, East Grinstead and Reigate garages received some new red RMLs on loan, pending the arrival of more green-painted examples. This view at West Croydon depicts Godstone's RML2287, about to penetrate deep into the Sussex countryside at Forest Row, on the edge of Ashdown Forest ('Winnie the Pooh' country). *David Hurdle*

Right: The Forest Row terminus of route 409 was in fact the railway station, on the forecourt of which RML2347 was photographed in October 1966. Route 409 was based on East Surrey's route S9 dating back to 1922, which ran from West Croydon all the way to Uckfield — a journey of 32 miles. When the LPTB took over in 1933 the route was cut back to Forest Row, which was still outside the LPTB's designated area but to which running powers were granted. *Marcus Eavis*

Left: Red buses dominate Reigate in May 1967 as Leyland Atlantean XA6 from East Grinstead garage passes RF328 on the Upper West Street stand. The Central Area XA was taking part in comparative trials with Country Area Daimler Fleetlines (XF class), this being the second time such an exchange had taken place (the first having been in 1965). The red RF, along with several others spread around the Country Area, was on loan to cover for the large number of green RFs undergoing overhaul simultaneously. *Roy Hobbs*

Above: Several RFs were still on loan on 1 January 1970, when LT was required to transfer responsibility for Country Area bus and Green Line coach operations to London Country Bus Services. The new company, which inherited vehicle shortages, gladly accepted the loan for a further period. RF374 is seen at Brockham Common, well known for its Guy Fawkes celebrations. *Roy Hobbs*

Left: In October 1965, during a lull between exchange trials with XAs, XF4 from East Grinstead garage climbs Bell Street, Reigate, on one of the few weekday short workings of route 424 to Woodhatch 'Beehive' (despite the destination shown). At the rear of the bus can be seen the former offices of the East Surrey Traction Co, on the corner of Lesbourne Road, alongside the old company's bus garage. *Roy Hobbs*

Above: Red and green stand together at Reigate 'Red Cross' in September 1967. XA15 is on loan to East Grinstead garage, having been exchanged with an XF for comparative trials, and is clearly a popular bus on this occasion, while RML2308 is running empty, possibly returning to Reigate garage in Lesbourne Road. *Roy Hobbs*

Left and above: Red and green stand apart, facing opposite directions but at the same location — the now demolished Holmesdale Inn at South Park, Reigate. Borrowed RF387 was photographed in March 1967, while indigenous RF693 is seen some two months later. Route 430 linked Redhill with Reigate (they are pretty much joined anyway!) but by an indirect route. *Roy Hobbs*

Left: Red and green stand together again, this time in Reigate High Street in October 1965. RF280 is on the circuitous 447 route linking Redhill with Merstham, while RML2297, on loan to Godstone garage, is heading for Bromley North station on route 410. This service had previously been operated by the lowbridge 'Godstone' STLs and then by RLHs. In November 1964 the offending bridge at Oxted was by-passed to permit the use of standard-height buses, but, by popular request, the original routeing was reinstated in May 1966 after the road was lowered. *Roy Hobbs*

Above: Reigate's cavernous garage (now closed but not totally demolished), as seen in the summer of 1967. In the foreground stands RT3127, behind which can be seen rows of green RTs, modernised Green Line RFs, a red RT and RF and a Surrey County Council mobile library. Readers can compare this view with the interior of Reigate garage in the 1930s as depicted in *Glory Days: Green Line*, published by Ian Allan in 2000. *Roy Hobbs*

Left: RT2012 climbs Reigate Road, alongside Nork Park, on Derby Day 1967, having brought racegoers from Morden Underground station to Epsom Downs. This section of road was not served by buses, either red or green, although the RT will shortly be turning into Tattenham Way and running along part of route 164A. The 'Morden Express' still operates on Derby Day, along with the other special service, route 406F from Epsom station. *Roy Hobbs*

Above: Route 80 from Tooting Broadway penetrated sufficiently far into the Country Area to disappear off the bottom of the Central Area map. In this view at Lower Kingswood in June 1969 RF537 is turning into Buckland Road from the Brighton Road — now a busy dual-carriageway leading to the M25 junction at the top of Reigate Hill. *Roy Hobbs*

Left: Buses left outside to freeze at Leatherhead garage in late 1969 include, from left to right, GS14, RF650, RF271 and RT3526. The diminutive Guy Special (GS) operated the sparsely used 416 service from Tadworth to Esher. Central Area route 65 from Ealing (Argyle Road) used to terminate at this garage, as subsequently did the 71 from Kingston. *Roy Hobbs*

Right: The frost at Leatherhead garage is nothing compared with the snow on Epsom racecourse in this wintry scene. RT2338 waits at the Tattenham Corner terminus (opposite the railway station) of route 164A, no doubt shortly to be passed by a green RT on the 406 service from Kingston to Redhill. *Roy Hobbs*

Left: Brand-new RML2311 stands proudly outside the former East Surrey garage at Godstone in October 1965. At this time Godstone also had new red Routemasters on loan. This was due to a shortage of the green variety, the requirement arising from new schedules reflecting economies gained as a result of the introduction of these larger buses. *Maurice Bateman*

Above: This rural setting is on the Metropolitan's Harrow-on-the-Hill–Uxbridge branch, which opened on 4 July 1904, with Met No 1 (L44) hauling the inaugural train. On 24 August 1969, to mark the centenary of the District Railway, which had commenced operations as the Metropolitan District Railway on Christmas Eve 1868, a special train formed of 'Q23', 'Q27' and 'Q31' clerestory-roofed stock was operated. The 'Centenarian' special, headed by 'Q23' No 4204, is seen near Hillingdon. *Marcus Eavis*

A Central Line train from Hainault to Woodford, composed of a pair of Cravens motor cars dating from 1960 with two pre-1938 trailers in between, seen near Chigwell in early 1964. The unit is undergoing trials for driverless operation prior to the introduction of automatic trains on the Victoria Line, which opened in 1968. *Marcus Eavis*

New surface stock of streamlined design first entered service in 1937 on the District Line. The flared body sides were not just cosmetic; the absence of external foot boards prevented passengers from hanging on to the outside of a moving train in an attempt to open the doors. In the summer of 1957 a set of this distinctive stock, heading for Richmond, leaves Gunnersbury, which station had been opened by the London & South Western Railway in 1869 as Brentford Road. Chiswick (bus) Works is in the background.
Marcus Eavis

Above: '2/6 [12½p] from Golders Green on the Northern Line, change at Camden Town', went the 1967 Top Twenty song entitled 'Finchley Central'. Ten years earlier a train of 1938 tube stock from High Barnet arrives at this former Great Northern Railway station. Opened in 1867 as Finchley & Hendon, the station was renamed Finchley (Church End) in 1894, becoming Finchley Central in 1940 when first used by Underground trains. *Marcus Eavis*

Right: District Railway 'F' stock entered service in 1920 and lasted until 1963, by which time the final examples were confined to the Met's Uxbridge branch and the East London Line. The stock was noted both for its rapid acceleration and, as a result of each carriage having three pairs of double doors (on each side), for shifting crowds. This evening shot in 1957 depicts two trains of 'F' stock on the East London Line near New Cross. *Phil Tatt*

43

Left: Acton Works, the central overhaul works for Underground trains, was built in 1922, at the same time as Chiswick (bus) Works, from which it was separated only by a railway line. This photograph, taken on 13 March 1964, shows, mounted on trucks, the bodies of a 1938 driving motor car, a 1927 trailer converted to run with 1938 stock and an Amersham 1960 ('A60') trailer. *E. J. McWatt / Online Transport Archive*

Above: This view of Acton Works, recorded from the service road behind Princes Avenue on 13 May 1965, shows a variety of Underground stock. In the foreground is a 1923 'G'-class ('Q23') motor car, one of 14 which owed their longevity to the fact that they were west-facing, whereas most of the more modern motor cars were east-facing. *Nick Lera*

Above: Acton Town station (named Mill Hill Park until 1910) on the District Line was rebuilt in its present form in 1932, when the Piccadilly Line was extended west of Hammersmith. This scene from 1957 shows a train of pre-1938 tube stock (standard stock built between 1923 and 1934), the last being withdrawn by LT in 1966 (and then sold to BR for use on the Isle of Wight!). *Marcus Eavis*

Right: From 1939 the South Acton shuttle was worked by one of two 1923 'G'-class cars converted for double-ended operation and deliberately bearing similar numbers (4167 and 4176) readily to distinguish them from normal single-ended motor cars. The shuttle is seen leaving Acton Town in 1957 to make its journey of less than ¾ mile. The service ceased on 28 February 1959, and the track was removed. *Marcus Eavis*

Left and right: The South Acton shuttle arrives at South Acton station in 1958. The Acton Loop Line, as it was known, was built in 1899 but was not opened for passengers until 1905, when electric trains began to operate from South Acton to Hounslow, with trains subsequently going also to South Harrow and Uxbridge. Originally double-track, the branch was singled in 1932 and the shuttle introduced following the extension of the Piccadilly Line and cessation of through trains on the Acton Loop. The line from Kew Bridge to Willesden Junction, which used to belong to the former North & South Western Junction Railway, can be seen in the background. *Phil Tatt*

Above: Class M1 trolleybus No 1530 travels along the upper end of Green Street, near Forest Gate, on its way from Walthamstow in 1958. Route 685 was a victim of Stage 5 of the trolleybus-abandonment programme, effected on 3 February 1960 and involving West Ham and Walthamstow depots. A new RM-operated bus service, route 58, replaced the 685. *Phil Tatt*

Right: Working route 693 through Ilford in 1958 is the last (numerically) of the 43 trolleybuses intended for South Africa and diverted to London in the period 1941-3 because of wartime risks to shipping. As a result of these vehicles' being non-standard, as well as requiring special dispensation to run because of their extra width and weight, the whole fleet was concentrated on one depot, Ilford. *Phil Tatt*

Above: Bicycles rule supreme in High Street, Barkingside, on an old-style Sunday morning in 1958. An RT on route 129 has just passed trolleybus No 1743 of the 'SA2' class, which, together with the 'SA1' class, comprised Leyland vehicles destined for Durban. Indeed, the upper portion of their side windows consisted of darkened glass to protect passengers from the hot sun (somewhat unnecessary in Britain!). Route 691 succumbed at the third stage of the trolleybus-abandonment programme, buses taking over on 19 August 1959 on new route 169. *Phil Tatt*

Right: Classified 'SA3', the intended Johannesburg trolleybuses, such as No 1761 on the stand at London Road, Barking, in 1958, were AEC vehicles. Continuing delays in the delivery of Routemasters meant that RTs and RTLs had again to be used for this stage of the trolleybus-abandonment programme — not ideal, considering the limited passenger capacity of these buses compared with the trolleybuses they were replacing (56 seats instead of 72) and the reduced eventual resale value of these otherwise surplus vehicles. *Phil Tatt*

Left: Route 669 from Stratford Broadway to North Woolwich succumbed to Stage 5 of the trolleybus-abandonment programme, being replaced by new bus route 69 from 3 February 1960. In 1958 'E1' No 582, a Brush-bodied AEC, travels along Albert Road towards North Woolwich railway station, with King George V Dock in the background. *Phil Tatt*

Above: West Ham depot 'N2' No 1656 looks resplendent standing on the cobbles at the North Woolwich terminus of route 669. The rounded side window at the front of the upper deck was a distinguishing feature of the Park Royal bodywork fitted to this class. *Phil Tatt*

55

Above: The first stage of the trolleybus-abandonment programme involved Carshalton and Bexleyheath depots, buses taking over from 4 March 1959. In this 1958 view, 'D2' Leyland No 468 stands at Bexleyheath Broadway on route 696 to Parsons Hill, Woolwich, in front of a terminating 698 trolleybus. *Phil Tatt*

Right: Some of Bexleyheath's trolleybuses were rebodied following serious bomb damage suffered by the depot during World War 2. In this 1958 view two of these rebuilds can be seen inside the depot: 'D2' No 405B and 'H1' No 799B, the 'B' signifying that the repairer was East Lancashire Coachbuilders. A comparison between these replacement bodies and the original body on 'D2' No 440 in the foreground reveals several differences. *Phil Tatt*

Left: The Central Line's Epping–Ongar branch in Essex was built by the Great Eastern Railway in 1865 and transferred to LT in 1935. There were two intermediate stations, one being North Weald, shown here in 1962, when the shuttle was worked by pre-1938 tube stock. *Marcus Eavis*

Above: Later in the 1960s the shuttle was in the hands of 1959 tube stock, as seen here at Blake Hall, the second intermediate station. This was LT's most under-used station, with only six passengers per day when it closed in 1981. North Weald and Ongar stations were closed by LT on 30 September 1994, when services ceased. *Marcus Eavis*

Left: Another view of North Weald, dating from 28 April 1962, with the Epping–Ongar shuttle looking decidedly grubby. The steam locomotive, hauling a railtour, is a Class J15 0-6-0, built, appropriately, by the Great Eastern Railway. *Nick Lera*

Above: Before the branch was electrified in 1957, BR provided a steam shuttle. Motive power was typically a Great Eastern Class F5 2-4-2 tank, and plans are afoot to construct a new one for the branch now that long-delayed plans to reopen the line have come to fruition. The first public service was run on 10 October 2004 between Ongar and North Weald using a DMU. 'F5' No 67203 stands alongside a Central Line service to West Ruislip in this view at Epping on 30 July 1956. *R. Becknese / Online Transport Archive*

Right: Former West Ham tram No 307, with an ex-East Ham vehicle behind, stands at the Ilford Broadway terminus of route 63 to Aldgate on 15 July 1939, less than two months before the outbreak of World War 2. *C. Carter*

Left: This view of the Victoria Embankment from Waterloo Bridge, with Somerset House in the background, was recorded during Last Tram Week in June/July 1952. The 'E3' tram, followed by an RTL bus, is using the sub-surface conduit system for electric power and is heading for Woolwich. *Jack Wyse*

Lower left: This tram has travelled over Westminster Bridge and failed to negotiate the curve onto the Victoria Embankment, alongside the RT bus on route 109. Help is at hand in the form of a large breakdown tender. *Jack Wyse*

Right: The 'C'-class trolleybuses were introduced in 1936 and were a familiar sight in the northwest suburbs until the last examples were withdrawn in November 1959. 'C3' No 290, complete with rear wheel spats, is seen in 1958 in the Harrow Road at Kensal Town on its return from Paddington Green to Sudbury. *Phil Tatt*

Left: LT's longest trolleybus route was the 630 from Harrow Road (Scrubs Lane) to West Croydon station via Putney Bridge. This service, operated from Hammersmith depot, was replaced under Stage 7 of the trolleybus-abandonment programme, buses taking over on 20 July 1960. 'K2' Leyland No 1158 is seen in July 1960 in Shepherd's Bush Road. *Martin Jenkins / Online Transport Archive*

Above: On the last day of London's trolleybuses, 8 May 1962, 'L3' No 1405 successfully avoids the old tramlines which used to protrude through the tarmac in London Road, Twickenham, on the section near the railway station. The author recalls a nasty experience when the wheels of his bicycle got stuck in the grooves! *Nick Lera*

Left: More associated with the 607 service through Ealing Broadway (which was the author's local trolleybus route), the 'F1' class, introduced in 1937, is represented here on route 628 in July 1960. The location is Fulham Palace Road, close to which was Bishop's Park School. Trolleybuses were noted for their rapid acceleration, which was unfortunate for one schoolgirl who, accompanied by some classmates, was taking home a filled casserole dish after a cookery lesson; as she climbed the stairs directly above the conductor, the lid slipped, allowing some gravy to spill onto his cap. Luckily, he wasn't aware … and no-one dared tell him! *Martin Jenkins / Online Transport Archive*

Right: Some trolleybuses met their end before the abandonment programme was implemented. Swingeing service cuts in 1955 and 1956 had rendered large numbers of trolleybuses redundant and, apart from some which had an extended life following sale to Malaya, the majority went for scrapping at Bird's of Stratford-upon-Avon, where this depressing photograph was taken in 1956. Among the carcases are three identifiable vehicles — 'C1s' Nos 177 and 182 and 'C2' No 247. *Neil Davenport*

Above: The final stage of the trolleybus-abandonment programme, implemented on 8 May 1962 and involving Isleworth and Fulwell depots, was not originally planned. However, the sale to Spain of all but two of the 'Q1' postwar trolleybuses, which were to have been retained for several years on the Kingston-area routes, could not be resisted. Following their departure older types were drafted in as short-term replacements; Class L3 No 1390 is depicted in Heath Road, Twickenham, on 24 March 1962.
Nick Lera

Right: Seen at Hampton Court, also on 24 March 1962, 'L3' No 1396 purports to be working route 605; in fact this service operated between Wimbledon and Teddington via Kingston, without serving Hampton Court.
Nick Lera

BRANDY make sure it's MARTELL

MOORES FOR FORD
Ford
WEYBRIDGE
and
SUNNINGDALE

Look ahead
and be assured
LONDON
AND
MANCHESTER

JACKSONS
OF
GARAGE
WEYBRIDGE Ltd

LONDON TRANSPORT

KYY
510

Left: Displaying its provincial body styling, RLH10 belonged to the first batch of 20 low-height AEC Regent IIIs, ordered by Midland General but diverted to LT in 1950. Allocated to Addlestone garage, it is seen outside the former station building at Staines West, terminus of lowbridge double-decker routes 436, 436A and 461. The station building, which started life as a private dwelling before the railway arrived, still survives, having been converted into smart-looking offices. *Maurice Bateman*

Right: On a dreary winter's day in 1969 RM77 and RT815 stand at the Aldgate terminus of their respective routes. RT operation of route 42 had only a few weeks to go, Merlin single-deckers taking over from 25 January 1970. *Roy Hobbs*

Left: By the time the last of the RTW class of 8ft-wide buses had been withdrawn from public service on 14 May 1966 they looked very down at heel. Surprisingly, those which were retained for training duties generally looked much better, as evidenced by RTW44 in February 1969 at Trafalgar Square, following a repaint. *Mike Harries*

Above: Examples of three major types seen in London in the 1950s, 1960s and 1970s congregate outside Golders Green Underground station in the autumn of 1969. From left to right are RT4539, RM2130 and RF368. Hendon garage lost its last RTs when route 183 was converted to DMS operation on 5 January 1975. *Roy Hobbs*

The roar of the Leyland engine would not be heard for much longer at Golders Green after this 1968 photograph of RTL1602 was taken. This vehicle was one of 13 still licensed for passenger service on the last day of RTL operation, 29 November 1968, which saw Willesden garage's routes 176 and 226 succumb to RT operation. RMs and an RF complete the picture, with RM2163 in the foreground. *Phil Tatt*

Most of the 76-strong RLH class of lowbridge double-deckers ran in the Country Area, but there were a few Central Area routes requiring double-deck capacity at a time when the only single-deckers available were 41-seat RFs. Thus Harrow Weald had RLHs for route 230, on which service RLH60 is seen approaching Northwick Park Underground station in the summer of 1968. *Phil Tatt*

Left: In the final summer of LT operation of Country Area routes, before these were transferred to London Country Bus Services, RT3002 is seen near King's Langley on its way from the LT outpost of Aylesbury in June 1969. *Dave Brown*

Right: In 1966/7 175 members of the RF class were modernised for continued Green Line operation. This photograph taken at Gatwick in September 1968 shows modernised RF47 working the prestigious 727 service from Luton to Crawley, linking Heathrow and Gatwick airports, which was introduced from 13 May 1967. *Mike Harries*

Above: From January 1956 the polished parts of wheels were painted over, so this study of Turnham Green garage's RT2577 resplendent at Chessington Zoo serves as a reminder of just how smart LT vehicles could look. In the background can be seen the embankment for BR's aborted Chessington-branch extension. *Harry Luff*

Right: Class N1 trolleybus No 1569 from Bow depot experiences route 663's short-lived extension from Ilford in this view recorded at the Chadwell Heath terminus. Behind stands a South African-type trolleybus on the 693. Both routes would be replaced by buses from 19 August 1959. *Harry Luff*

Above: For those who bought the author's previous LT book, *London Transport in Exile*, here is the missing STL! Operated by LT from 1937 to 1953, STL1836 then served with T. Canham (Services) of Whittlesey, Cambridgeshire, until 1960, being seen the previous year in Peterborough bus station. *Harry Luff*

Back cover: The last day of London's trams (before their reintroduction in the Croydon area in May 2000) was 5 July 1952. On this memorable date 'E3' No 165 was photographed at Lee Green, between Lewisham and Eltham, working route 46 to Beresford Square, Woolwich. *Neil Davenport*